Sequel to Slumber

Finding a New Path with Encouragement, Strength and Love

Michaela Hackman

Awakening

Sometimes you awake from a dream
Wonder where you are
And realize you were sleeping

Sometimes you awake from sleeping
Wonder where you are
And realize you weren't living

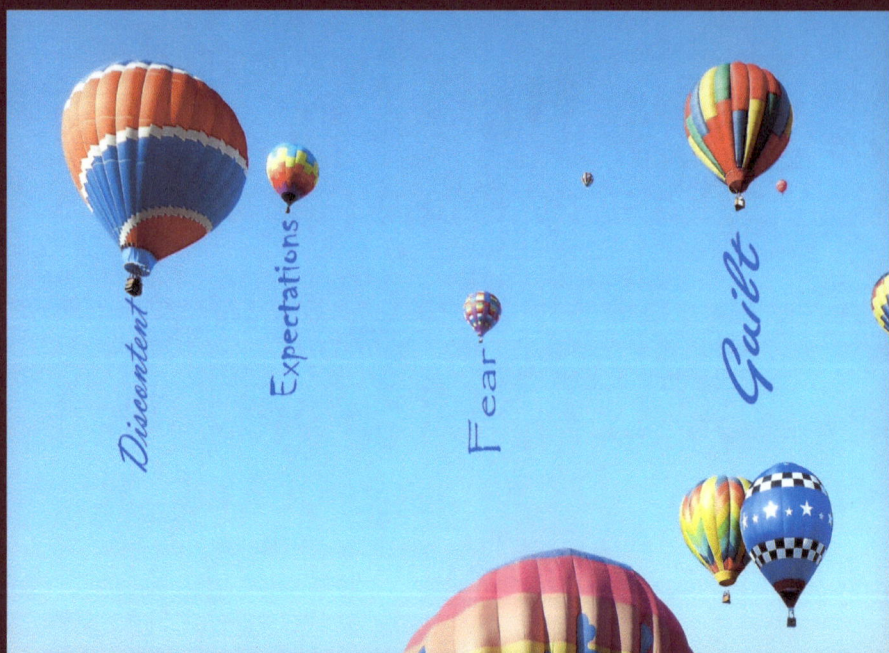

It is amazing
What your heart is capable of
Once your soul has been set free!

Peace...

Love....

Happiness...

Dreams...

Bloom where you are planted,
Take root and you will grow.
You are meant to be here right now,
And today is all we know.
Sow seeds of understanding, compassion,
Truth and love.
And let it all be watered
With rain sent from above.
Your life will be abundant,
Ever growing, full and bright.
If you will bloom where you are planted,
And accept God's good and
gracious light.

I can't change yesterday.
It may have been the road
that got me to today.
And even though it was filled with
detours and potholes
and road signs that made the journey long,
I embrace the joy along the way that made
my life blessed.

Tomorrow isn't here yet.
It may be where I'm headed,
but even with a perfectly mapped out
route, there could be obstacles that
keep me from arriving.

The present is all I have.
And a present it is.
I will open each day with a grateful smile.
I will live each moment
as if it is the best gift I have ever received.

This is my road.

I'm really not too worried
About how you interpret my truth.
If you respect me as a person,
You will accept me as I am.
Because judging without understanding
Says more about how you feel towards yourself
Than it could ever say
About how you feel towards me.

Water from mountains

Flowing to places unknown

Falling isn't bad

Why do I stand here frozen?
Afraid to say a word
Worried I'll be judged

If you only knew who I am
You would think...
...I am kind
...I am funny
...I am loving
...I am smart
But I'm not so sure...

Why do I give you all of that power?
Why do I think your eyes
Matter more than my own?
Why isn't it enough that I believe in myself?

I'm not looking at you through such critical eyes
Why should I think you look at me that way?

Maybe you feel the same.

A friend indeed you will always be
Whenever I need help
With the world I see.

A friend to you I promise, too
You can count on that
In all you do.

Letting Go

I feel your hands around my neck
I can't breathe
You are choking me

I gasp for air
Your grip closes my throat tight
I try to fight

I can't scream
I can't get away
There is nothing I can say

I try to tell you to stop
You won't let go
The words of my voice will not flow

I can't see you, can you see my fear?
Am I really here ?

I just want to be heard
My words are my truth
I don't speak them to hurt you

Let me get out the words
Just let me say what I need to say
And don't make me die for my words either way

Why won't you let me speak!
I fight for air
As I struggle I catch a glimpse in the mirror

I freeze at the reflection
Of the person I see
I'm doing this to myself, I'm choking me!

He judged my soul
Without ever showing his own
Not enough
Never enough
What is enough?

Enough!
Taking the gavel back into my own hands
I tapped his skin to awaken his soul
But he shattered into a million pieces
Revealing his nothingness
His emptiness

I swept up only the pieces of myself
He had chipped away and taken from me
Carefully discarding those I no longer needed
Placing back those I had missed
Making new ones
To complete the puzzle I had become

In a new light I awoke
To ever changing color and reflection
In each perfectly crafted piece
Creating a magnificently imperfect me

Your words are shallow...
Like the wind
That can't be captured and described

Your words have no meaning...
But can be felt
Like the treacherous force of a hurricane
When you speak

All that is left when you stop
Is the damage left behind...
Ripped hearts...
Tattered souls...

I need to find a soft breeze
With gentle words
That blow through my hair...
Tickles my skin...
Enlightens my soul...
Warms my heart...

I can't change the force with which you blow

It's time to put on my windbreaker
It's time for me to go

HER BROKEN SOUL WEPT
WHEN HIS EMPTY SOUL LEFT
TEARS OF HAPPINESS

Each day a gift is offered, a present in itself
But I let it sit, fearing it, I let it sit on a shelf

The present is wrapped in fear
Torn with anxiety
Stained with discontent from the past
Taped shut with expectations
Tied in ribbons of guilt
Feelings and thoughts that continue to last

I struggle to open the present
It's hard to get past the packaging
I set it aside for another day
Hoping the wrapping will go away

Afraid to add to emotions it carries
Nervous to face the feelings long sown
Not convinced that anything inside
Could ever be any better than what I've known

It won't measure up to be the best it could be
And the ribbons will tangle unless I stop me
From not thinking there's more I somehow could do
To make my life better, and shiny, and new

It's easier to walk away in despair
Than to think that the world could ever be fair
And let me be happy, like a new present seemed
With shiny new hope, new love and new dreams

With all the feelings that keep me from living
I relive each day with a new present giving
My thoughts keep the present wrapped too tight
And I give in another day instead of fight
Because I can't let myself see what's inside
Held back by my past, my future denied

The present sits patient and patiently waits
And tempts me, pleasingly, with a new fate
I know I must work at letting go
Of the pain in my past that I used to know
I deserve that present unwrapped of the past
Do I dare to take it now?
Do I dare to make it last?

One day I'll wake up
The present will be gone
My body once free
Will forever be
Wrapped in regret for eternity

How do I let go of the self-pity
And forgive myself for all the wasted years
Of hiding deep inside myself
And holding back the tears

I kept hoping it would all just change
That my life would be just fine
I didn't understand that I was wasting time

I couldn't change a thing
No matter how I tried
To think I lived a life of love was living one big lie

I wasn't unlovable, that wasn't it
I had so much to give
But each day became a struggle
And I wasn't able to live...

....a life filled with love, acceptance and respect
I fought to hold on to everything
And gave up all that I expect

But that isn't how I live anymore
I finally broke those ties
I get to write out the next chapter in my life
And I need to do so before time flies

I'm holding back and hiding
Without a reason why
I need to find a way
To tell the past goodbye
To relax and let a new life happen
...It's not like I didn't try

I can hide...I can flow...
I can fly up in the sky...
What difference will it make to you...
I'm the one who should get to choose
To fly my course the way I see...
To flow in a pattern other
Than what's expected of me
To hide from what everyone wants me to be

I can fly...I can flow...
I can hide from it all...
What difference will it make to me ...
If you choose to not want to see
The beauty that will always be...
The truth of me just being me

Excuse me Sir, can you help me?
I'm looking for my twin
I haven't seen her in many years
I don't even know where to begin.

What's that, you ask? Can I describe her?
Well, she stands about this tall
In the summer her hair is a bit light blond
But it's back to brown by fall.

She has kind eyes and a warm heart
And is a bit funny in a sarcastic way

She can cook, she can clean, she can climb a mountain top
And do it all in a day.

She's a friend, she's a giver, never a taker
She would never want to break a heart
She works hard, takes pride, excels in all that she does
She finishes all that she starts.

She left a long time ago...
Well actually no, that isn't true
Her body was here going through the motions
But her soul was black and blue.

She has achieved much success in the world
But there's one thing she still seeks to find
And that's what it feels like to be deeply loved
Body, soul and mind.

So, kind Sir, can you help? Have you seen my twin?
The man held up a mirror and said
"Who you seek is there, within.

For if you care enough about the world
And all that is in it, the love you seek will find you
Once you believe you deserve to be in it.

So I say to you, dear girl, dear twin
You're one, you are the same
Once you see the best in her is YOU
You will have your flame.

Your flame will burn with fire
Lit from passion in your soul.
And love will be drawn to your warmth
As you will have paid your toll.

When you know your own true worth
You will attract the right kind
Don't settle for less than someone
Who will love you body, soul and mind.

So don't give up, dear girl
Take this mirror to help you see
The wonderful woman looking back
And know that you are free."

Floating in the air
Not willing to look back down
The chance for a new beginning
Is music with a new sound

I get to choose what song I sing next
Which direction I want to fly
Exciting and scary at the same time
I should not be afraid to try

To pilot my life without a map
New directions and new plans
I'll decide along the way
Where I intend to land

Do I dare to cut the tethered ties
That keep me from being free
Do I stop being the one who does
What everyone expects of me

I want to take off and experience all
That I know down deep in my heart
Will bring me joy and peace and love
And strengthen every part

My soul, my body, my mind set free
Free to fly away
The time for living is time right now
No time to wait for the right day!

Breezy Day

Zipping Along

We grow up into a world
With coloring books on a shelf
We're expected to choose one
Designed by someone else

A standard issue box of crayons
With a rainbow of colors

Color inside the lines
vivid and bright
And be like all the others
But it's all so one dimensional,
over time the colors fade
The lines blur.......our dreams go away

I went back to the shelf
To find something new
The first one I had chosen
left me blank, empty, and blue

I stood there flipping pages,
not seeing what I wanted to see
I realized these books
weren't meant to let me be
the me I wanted to be

I left that shelf and searched for a
notebook, clean and clear
And decided from that day on
I'll make my own path appear.

I am meant to be a butterfly
If I believe I can fly
I can fly
But my wings have not yet emerged

Patiently waiting
My evolution still in progress
I began in the comfort of my mother's safe arms
Then to a rebellious cocoon
Of awkward growth and trying to belong

Once thinking I found myself
Catipilling my way through time
Giving up the hope
That I was ever meant to have wings

Then one day it was time
Unparalleled transformation
A new life began

The hardened shell of my life
Gave time for the colors of my wings to deepen
As chips began to fall away from the cracked shell
The imperial colors of a butterfly
Waiting to be revealed on open wings
Began to emerge
...Beautiful
...Free
...Transcendent

I spread my new wings
No longer waiting to fly
And head into life awaiting in the sky
I am a butterfly

Will I be satisfied with today if I don't get to see tomorrow?
Will I have said and done all that I want,
Or will I need more time to borrow?

Time isn't a promise, it's not earned in trade for a thing
Have I spent the time given to me
Well enough to feel I bring...

Joy to the faces of others, laughter to the lives of all
Compassion to the souls who need it,
And have I done it standing tall?

If I don't get to see tomorrow, will I feel settled from my past?
Or will I carry those burdens to eternity to forever last?

Am I making a difference in the lives
Of those I meet along the way?
Do I remember to tell them how much they mean,
Or is there more that I should say?

Have I walked away from those who will only bring me pain?
And do I surround myself with those
From whose love I have much to gain?

I must make peace with myself now,
Peace before it is too late
And live my life without regret
Before I stand at Heaven's gate.

Do you see me?
Or am I invisible
Like the tree
You hardly see
That stands here faithfully

Changing seasons always the same
Losing pieces only in storms

I'm here to shelter you
With shade from the burning sun

You hesitate to pick me up when I fall
Even though there are times I cannot help it at all

Left feeling invisible
I lie dormant in wintery discontent

Until I find a glimmer of hope
That makes me want to bloom again

You needing me
So you breathe life into me
But still not really seeing me

If you could only see
Every time you look at me
The beauty I bring to your life
Like the petals of blooms on a spring tree

If you could only see
Every time you look at me
The light that glimmers in my eyes
The way the sun gleams from the sky
Through leaves of a tree on a summer's day

If you could only see
Every time you look at me
All the colors of my love
Given to you bountifully
Like the majestic leaves
As they fall from trees

If you could only see
Every time you look at me
The coldness in my solitude
The brittleness in my spirit
As I await
For you to notice that I am here
Like a tree in winter
Ready to bloom once more
Before I become a hollow core

Music in the background in one ear
The ocean waves crashing on the sand in the other
The sun on my face
The breeze in my hair...
... I could be anywhere

But here is where I need to be
To remind myself of how I see
My life the way I want it to be
And wonder what is stopping me

My life has changed
I'm not the same girl I used to be
I'll take the good
Leave the bad behind
And explore my life and all there is to see

Tomorrow isn't defined by yesterday
It hasn't even begun
But what I do today will set the path
For the rise of a beautiful sun

Still paralyzed by fear...
Why am I so afraid?
It didn't all turn out as I planned
Doesn't mean I can't be brave

And define tomorrow with no chains that bind
And seek to find
Everything that fills my mind

And touches my soul
And warms my heart
And makes me feel alive
And be willing to live one moment at a time

What would I do if I had no fear?
Regardless of whether the end of time was near?
There is nothing in this world that should be left undone
If I think it and do it then I will have won

And if something doesn't turn out quite as I thought
The journey will bring me the answers I sought
If I listen closely to the voice in my heart
What I dream and reality will never be apart

Moving On

What if we viewed love like we do the sun?
Each morning we're graced with the beauty
Of its entrance into our world
As it offers a painted sky
That is different from the days past
Curious as to how it will affect our day
Sad when it doesn't show up
But comforted to know it's only behind a cloud
In awe of its mid-day brilliance
And ability to provide warmth and help things grow
Inspired by its majestic setting and the peacefulness it brings
Knowing it will return tomorrow.
Could love be that simple?

Will you show me gardens where magic comes alive...

Where there are blooms of lace
and fairies dance under shaded leaves...

Will you dance in your mind as you look in my eyes...

Will you feel the linger of my lips long after we part...

Will you smile at the idea that this is only the start?

Why is this so hard?
Girl meets boy, boy meets girl

We start along on the right track
We swear we won't look back

We begin the path just fine
But there's fear in the back of our mind
We feel the fear of an oncoming train
Afraid our hearts will feel the strain

Others before us laid these rails
We still look upon raised nails
In the planks as if we failed
Afraid the truth will somehow tell

A story we still don't want to face
As if our life is some type of race

To the finish without being alone
But how could we have known

How hard this was going to be
To expose all of our vulnerabilities
To let you be the you you need to be
To let me be me and for us to both be free

To be who we are and not convert
We want love but our heart stays on alert
Why can't we just erase all our past hurt
Box it up and bury in the dirt

And swear we won't look back
And start along on the right track

Boy meets girl, girl meets boy
Why is this so hard?

Walk with me along this path
Of lost dreams and broken promises
Along the way we just might find
A love that will treat us kind
And a friendship that won't be left behind

We may need to reach a hand to each other
In case we stumble a bit along the way
If we don't always chose the right words to say
Let's not carrying those burdens into the next day

We can't be sure where this path will lead
But life is too short to worry too much
Let's not let our past be used as a crutch
To keep us from enjoying a touch

Leave your fears behind and walk beside me
We'll discover a life too beautiful not to share
We'll discover what it means to truly care
Let's not be afraid to take this dare

The destination can't be promised
But this I promise you
I'll treasure your heart in all that I do
And let fate and love see us through

This path will become our own
Fresh promises and new dreams
Life will be as it seems
And grace us with love redeemed

I think of you and wonder
Are you all that you say you are?
You rose to the top from up under
I consider you from afar

You want me now, a challenge you say
Your skills are sharp and quick
But if you win my heart one day
Will you keep a flame on the wick?

I don't want to hand my trusting heart
To a man who is unfit
I ask God to put my tender heart
In the hands of a man who deserves it

Is that a challenge you're up to
Or are we in this just for fun?
Will you let me fall slowly for you
Then embrace me when you've won?

Will I be the prize you dreamed of
Will you cherish me every day?
Is your heart truly ready for love
Or will you only chase it away?

I'll take all the time the Lord will give
To make sure that this is right
Because once I love I want to live
With my love forever in my sight

So consider this as we head
On this unfamiliar journey
I'm hearing all that you have said

If you've heard me,
Take my hand,
And I will not worry.

Threading your soul to mine
A needle moves through us with each motion
Entwining our bodies
Spinning our souls
Releasing raw emotion

The fabric we create
Gives us the comfort that we seek
It wraps us in a warmth of love
Ascending us to our peak

But fear pulls sharply at the threads
Threatening to unweave
All that we seek in each other
All that we believe

We chose a spool of thread too early
Not accounting for its length
Somewhere along the line
That short twine lost its strength

Our time has come to an impasse
The fibers bind our soul but not our mind
Our hearts beat in a different rhythm
Unsure of what in the future we will find

Will you take my end and tie it to yours
Or will you watch me break away
With our love left hanging by a thread
Leaving both of our ends to fray

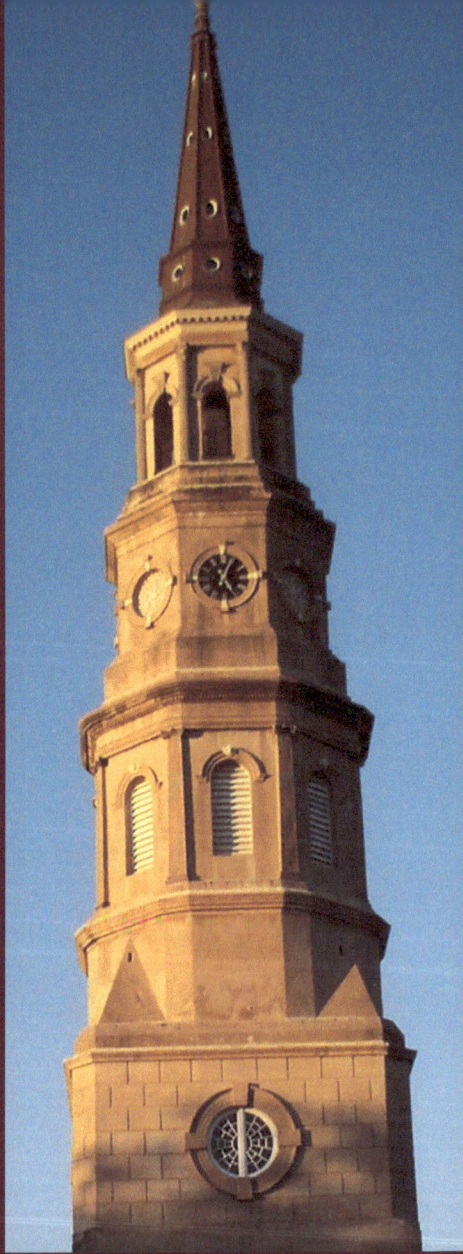

You stand here at arm's length from me.
I keep waiting for you to pull me in
And take me in your arms and say you never want to let me go.
But waiting for it isn't making it so.

All the while it isn't happening, I'm not living.
I'm waiting, my time I keep on giving.

I'm letting time stand still.
Except what will happen when I finally stop waiting
Is I will realize time never really did stand still.

It passed me by and I will be no further along
In my quest to share my life with someone
I will only have less to go on.

I want to use the ticking moments wisely,
As it passes I want love in my life to grow.
And I want to know that when I look back
I will see that I have gained so much and come so far.
But when I look back now,
I only see days fall off the calendar of my life
I look ahead and can't see clearly how many more are to come.

In all these days yet to come, I don't want to be afraid of anything
Because being afraid is paralyzing. It makes time stand still in my mind
But for real its days left behind.

I want to be so busy living and loving
That I don't even hear the ticking days fall as they will
Because only then will I be satisfied that I spent those days well.

I can't stand here any longer waiting
We can walk through this clock of days together
Or we can move through the moments alone
But if I go alone, understand that I can't look back
Because every time I look back and see you still standing there
I will wish you were right here.
I will be sadden to see someone who could have been right
Pining for a love that can't be
I don't want to carry that longing with me,
I need to travel light

Will you dance with me?
Neither of us has heard music for so long
In our hearts we hear the tune of a song
But we won't turn it up, we have too much fear
Afraid that the words won't be what we want to hear

But dancing isn't about one certain tune
All light and fluffy as we move about the room
The rhythm can change at any given turn
It doesn't mean the new dance will burn

There will be times when our songs will be in contrast
Especially if we keeping singing songs of our past
Leaving the purpose of the dance to only be lost
And signals for our timing to only get crossed

Let me take your hand and move to a new melody
Your ears will hear but you must let your heart see
The beauty of our movement as we move across the floor
And don't be afraid to let your heart crave more

Put one hand in mine and the other on my waist
Our faces together with lips close enough to taste
The sound of the music makes our senses come alive
As our bodies move in rhythm, our fears are washed aside

The songs are meant to release every feeling
Some happy, some sad, but all of them healing
We will move through this world dancing to our songs
Whether you lead or I, we will keep our dance strong

And when there are times your song has you blue
Just put your feet on mine and I will carry you
Until you get to a place where you can change the song
I'll dance with you there no matter how long

I know you would do the same for me
That's what dancing together should be
We're missing the music as we stand here and wait
We weren't meant to dance alone, that isn't our fate

I can't promise you our dance will always be in harmony
But if you accept that as part of life you will see
No one in this world will dance with you as well as me
So I'm asking you once more, will you dance with me?

A flower blooms
Her true color unknown
Until she knows herself

www.ingramcontent.com/pod-product-compliance
Lightning Source LLC
LaVergne TN
LVHW010026070426
835510LV00001B/8